Christmas

COLORING BOOK

Jessica Mazurkiewicz

DOVER PUBLICATIONS, INC.
MINEOLA, NEW YORK

Bibliographical Note

Christmas Coloring Book: Your Passport to Calm is a new work, first published by
Dover Publications, Inc., in 2017.

International Standard Book Number
ISBN-13: 978-0-486-81381-3
ISBN-10: 0-486-81381-9

Manufactured in China by RR Donnelley
81381901   2017
www.doverpublications.com

bliss

\\'blis\\

noun

1. supreme happiness; utter joy or contentment

2. heaven; paradise

3. your passport to calm

Take a pleasant journey to a world of relaxation with *BLISS Christmas Coloring Book: Your Passport to Calm.* Yuletide images include bows and packages, Christmas trees, gingerbread houses, mistletoe, mittens, snowmen, and other holiday tableaus. Many of the designs are sprinkled with words and phrases of the season: Deck the Halls, Let It Snow, Ho Ho Ho, Peace, Hope, Believe, and more, sure to help you to get in the spirit for this magical time of the year. Now you can travel to your newly found retreat of peace and serenity whenever you'd like with this petite-sized collection of sophisticated artwork.

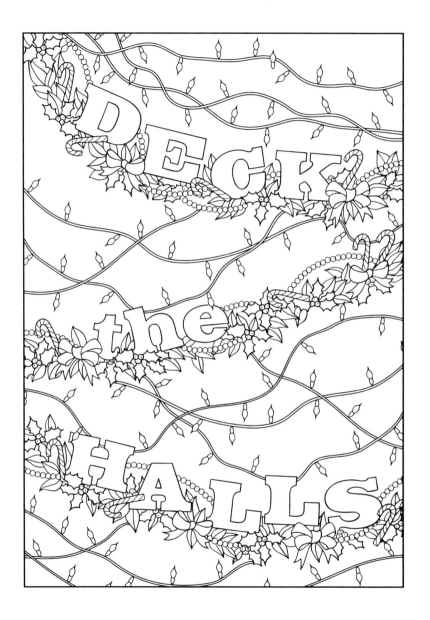

Merry Kissmas!

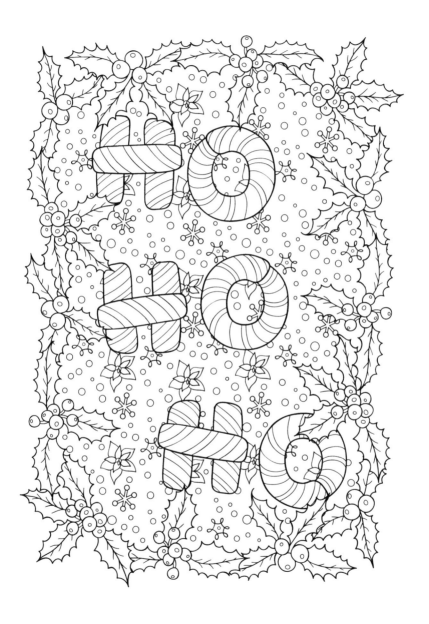

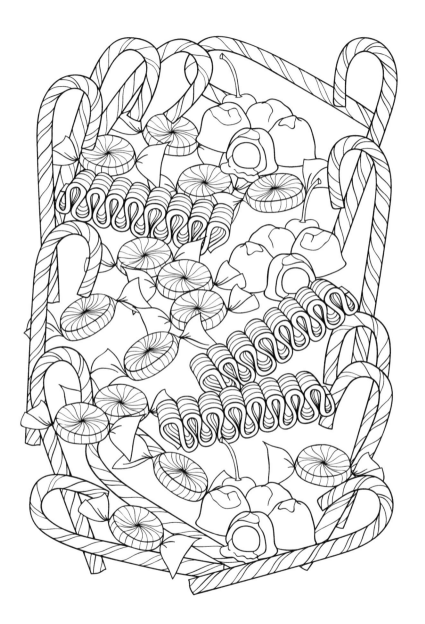